Are The Medjugorje Apparitions Authentic?

Theological Facts
And First Hand Accounts
Concerning the Apparitions
Of The Blessed Virgin Mary
At Medjugorje

**By DR. MARK MIRAVALLE
AND
WAYNE WEIBLE**

OTHER BOOKS BY DR. MARK MIRAVALLE

The Message of Medjugorje: The Marian Message to the Modern World (University Press of America, 1985)

Heart of the Message of Medjugorje (Franciscan University Press, 1988)

Medjugorje and the Family, Helping Families to Live the Message (Franciscan University Press, 1991)

Mary: Co-redemptrix, Mediatrix, Advocate (Queenship Publishing 1993)

Mary Co-redemptrix, Mediatrix, Advocate: Theological Foundations (Queenship Publishing, 1995)

Mary Co-redemptrix, Mediatrix, Advocate: Theological Foundations II (Queenship Publishing, 1997)

The Dogma and the Triumph (Queenship Publishing, 1998)

Contemporary Insights on a Fifth Marian Dogma: Mary Co-redemptrix, Mediatrix, Advocate, Theological Foundations III (Queenship Publishing, 2000)

Mary Co-redemptrix: Doctrinal Issues Today (Queenship Publishing, 2002)

Present Ecclesial Status of Devotion to St Philomena (Queenship Publishing, 2002)

In Continued Dialogue with the Czestochowa Commission (Queenship Publishing, 2002)

"With Jesus": The Story of Mary Co-redemptrix (Queenship Publishing, 2003)

Introduction to Mary: The Heart of Marian Doctrine and Devotion (Queenship Publishing, 2006)

Private Revelation: Discerning with the Church (Queenship Publishing, 2007)

The Seven Sorrows of China (Queenship Publishing, 2007)

Meet Mary: Getting to Know the Mother of God (Sophia Institute Press, 2008)

OTHER BOOKS BY WAYNE WEIBLE

Miracle at Medjugorje (Tabloid, Weible Columns, Inc., 1986)

Medjugorje: The Message (Paraclete Press 1989)

Letters from Medjugorje (Paraclete Press 1991)

Medjugorje: The Mission (Paraclete Press 1993)

The Final Harvest: Medjugorje at the end of the Century (Paraclete Press, 1999)

Final Harvest Revised (CMJ Marian Pub. 2003)

A Child Shall Lead Them (Paraclete Press 2005)

The Medjugorje Prayer Book (Paraclete Press 2007)

The Medjugorje Fasting Book (New Hope Press, due by fall 2008)

Are The Medjugorje Apparitions Authentic?

Are The Medjugorje Apparitions Authentic?

2008 First Printing

Copyright 2008 by Mark Miravalle and Wayne Weible

ISBN: 13 978-0-9820407-0-6
Library of Congress Cataloging-in-Publication Data: Applied for

Mark Miravalle

Wayne Weible

10 9 8 7 6 5 4 3 2 1

Published by New Hope Press
Hiawassee, Georgia
www.newhopepresspub.com
Printed in the United States of America

Net proceeds from the sale of this work will be donated to the international charity St. Joseph & The Helpers, formed to assist the people of Bosnia-Hercegovina, as well as other designated charities.

Are The Medjugorje Apparitions Authentic?

Theological Facts
And First Hand Accounts
Concerning the Apparitions
Of The Blessed Virgin Mary
At Medjugorje

By DR. MARK MIRAVALLE
AND
WAYNE WEIBLE

NEW HOPE
PRESS

P. O. Box 10 Hiawassee, GA. 30546
1-877-896-6061
www.newhopepresspub.com

INTRODUCTION

Reported apparitions of the Blessed Virgin Mary in the little village of Medjugorje in Bosnia-Herzegovina, one of six republics that comprised former Yugoslavia, have attracted the attention of the world and approximately 40 million pilgrims. Since June 24, 1981, six teenagers began to report daily visits from a heavenly entity, a beautiful young woman who identified herself as the Blessed Virgin Mary and said she came as the "Queen of Peace."

Three of the young people, all of whom are now adults, married and with children of their own, continue to report receiving apparitions from the Blessed Virgin Mary. She has allegedly appeared daily to the visionaries for more than 27 years. In that time, more than 40 million people from all over the world have come to the village on pilgrimage to see for themselves.

Spiritual conversion has been a consistent good fruit. But questions continue:

Is the phenomenon of the Medjugorje apparitions real?
Are these authentic apparitions of the Virgin Mary?
What is the official position of the Catholic Church about their authenticity?
Could these simply be the fraudulent deception of hysteric children (now adults) for reasons of attention and personal gain?

These and other questions concerning the reported Medjugorje phenomena have circulated in international newspapers, chancery offices, rectories and convents, and at family dining rooms the world over.

Five issues stand out from the great number of Medjugorje-related topics, as the "FAQs," the most frequently asked questions. In Part One, Dr. Mark Miravalle, Professor of Theology and Mariology at the Franciscan University of Steubenville, USA, will discuss these five questions from the perspective of the Catholic

Church's approach to Marian apparitions and the facts specific to the reported Medjugorje event. An internationally known lecturer in Mariology and author and editor of over 20 books in the area of Marian studies, Dr. Miravalle will engage these common questions/objections from an objectively theological and factual basis.

In Part Two, Wayne Weible, international writer and speaker on the apparitions, will convey various first-hand accounts of personal experiences of Medjugorje by just a few of those 40 million-plus pilgrims who have made the journey there to see for themselves. A former newspaper journalist, he has authored seven books about the apparitions, written hundreds of articles and has traveled to Medjugorje more than 90 times. He is well acquainted with the visionaries, the Franciscan priests in charge of the local parish and many of the Medjugorje villagers.

The sole purpose here is to answer the basic questions and give witness to the good fruits from what has been reportedly occurring in the Village of Medjugorje for close to three decades. There are numerous sources of material on the apparitions that can be found in book stores and on the internet, with literally hundreds of web sites.

PART ONE: THE THEOLOGY

THE CRITERIA
FOR DISCERNING APPARITIONS

-╀-

When the Catholic Church examines a reported Marian apparition, it uses criteria which can generally be summarized in three fundamental categories in order to discern authenticity from falsity.

First, it examines the reported message contents, asking the question: Is the reported message in conformity with the faith and moral teachings of the Catholic Church's Magisterium? The Holy Spirit, who guides the Church infallibly in truth on the domains of faith and morals, would never inspire a message to a private individual which is contrary to official Church teaching.

Secondly, the Church examines all reported phenomena relative to the reported apparition. For example, does the reported visionary experience a state of ecstasy during the alleged apparition, where the individual in some sense experiences a suspension of their external senses in light of the presence of the supernatural being? The category of phenomena would include all events proximate to the reported apparition which are inexplicable only through supernatural intervention.

The third criterion for authenticity is the spiritual fruits which derive from the reported apparition. This is the scriptural discernment Jesus offers us in the Gospel, that "you will know a tree by its fruits" (Mt. 7:17-20). For example, are there numerous examples of lasting conversion and return to the prayer and sacramental life of the Church? Are there long confession lines, coupled with a new zeal to live the Christian life of holiness according to the person's vocation and state in life? Are pilgrims coming from international sectors to pray at the reported site? Are there a significant number of priests and religious that have also visited the reported site, let alone bishops, on a personal basis?

The Church combines these three criteria to form an overall

assessment of whether or not there is evidence of authentic supernatural activity at the reported site. Let us see how these three criteria naturally manifest themselves in the following five questions
and objections regarding the events at Medjugorje.

CHURCH'S OFFICIAL POSITION

Question One: What is the official position of the Catholic Church regarding Medjugorje? Would it be an act of disobedience to pilgrimage to Medjugorje before the Church has given the apparitions a final and definitive approval?

On April 10, 1991, the Bishops' Conference of former Yugoslavia issued the "Declaration of the Ex-Yugoslavia Bishops' Conference on Medjugorje." The declaration neither approves nor condemns the apparitions, but does permit personal belief in the apparitions and personal pilgrimages to Medjugorje while the Church investigation continues.

The declaration makes clear that while at that particular point in the investigation "it cannot be affirmed that one is dealing with supernatural apparitions and revelations," it continues to state that "the faithful journeying to Medjugorje, prompted both by motives of belief and other motives, require attention and pastoral care."[1]

The Medjugorje apparitions are presently neither officially approved by the Church as being of supernatural origin *(constat de supernaturalitate)*; nor are they condemned by the Church as being false or invalid *(constat de non supernaturalitate)*. They are, at this point, in a type of middle category of evaluation referred to as *non constat de supernaturalitate,* which allows for personal belief in the authenticity of the apparitions along with personal (non-diocesan sponsored) pilgrimages to the apparition site, while the Church's official investigation is ongoing.

The Vatican Congregation for the Doctrine of the Faith (CDF), the Church's highest authority under the Pope himself for dealing with private revelation, confirmed the legitimacy of per-

---

1 *Declaration of the Ex-Yugoslavia Bishops' Conference on Medjugorje,* Ex-Yugoslavia Conference of Catholic Bishops, Zadar, April 10, 1991.

sonal belief and pilgrimages to Medjugorje at this point in the Church's evaluation in its statement issued on May 26, 1998 (Protocol No. 154/81-06419). In the statement of Archbishop Tarcisio Bertone, Secretary to the Prefect, Cardinal Joseph Ratzinger, given to French Bishop Monsignor (Msgr). Gilbert Aubrey, Archbishop Bertone confirmed that the 1991 Zadar statement was presently the official position of the Church regarding Medjugorje. Archbishop Bertone (presently, Cardinal Bertone, Secretary of State) stated: "As for the credibility of the 'apparitions' in question, this Dicastery respects what was decided by the bishops of the former Yugoslavia in the Declaration of Zadar, April 10, 1991."[2]

The 1998 CDF Statement on Medjugorje also makes specific reference to the personally negative position of the present local bishop of Mostar, Msgr. Ratko Peric, as constituting "what is and remains his personal opinion."[3]

It is important, therefore, to understand clearly the Vatican Congregation with the highest authority under the Roman pontiff on the issue of the apparitions directly states that the present bishop's personal position *is not the official position of the Church on Medjugorje.*

The CDF rather confirms the 1991 declaration of the ex-Yugoslavia Bishops as the present official position of the Church on Medjugorje, which in no way condemns the apparitions, but on the contrary allows for personal belief before any final decision is reached. The Vatican statement ends by likewise repeating the Church's expressed permission for private pilgrimages to Medjugorje while further investigation takes place.[4]

In August 2006, Cardinal Vinko Puljic of Sarajevo announced that a new commission of investigation would be formed to continue the ecclesiastical process of evaluation of Medjugorje. The Commission would operate under the direction of the Conference of Bosnian bishops and with the direct intervention of the Vatican

---

2 Archbishop Tarcisio Bertone, *Congregation for the Doctrine of the Faith, May 26, 1998 Statement to Msgr. Gilbert Aubry,* Protocol No. 154/81-06419, Vatican City.
3 Ibid.
4 Ibid.

CDF Congregation, and *not under the direct supervision of the local bishop.*[5]

In April 2008, the Vatican's authoritative involvement in the evaluation process was confirmed by the public statement of Msgr. Mato Zovkic, spokesperson of Cardinal Puljic, when he stated that the commission would not proceed until directions were given specifically by the Holy See.

5 Announcement of Cardinal Puljic of Sarajevo, Bosnia- Herzegovina, July 25, 1996, *Catholic News Service.*

DISOBEDIENCE?

Question Two: I have heard that there may have been acts of disobedience by the Franciscan priests at St. James Parish in Medjugorje against their local bishop. Is this true, and if so, how could Our Lady ever "bless" acts of disobedience by appearing there?

As we saw in the 1998 Vatican CDF statement on Medjugorje, the present local bishop's personal stance against Medjugorje is not the official position of the Church, and therefore it is most legitimate for a member of the Church to have personal belief in Medjugorje's authenticity until the Church completes its final evaluation. This permission, once again, is granted by the authoritative teaching of the Holy See and the former Yugoslavian Bishops' 1991 statement. The permission to personally believe in Medjugorje would of course include any of the Franciscan priests in Medjugorje who choose to give their own personal assent to the apparitions.

To claim, therefore, that some Franciscan priests are acting in "disobedience" to the local bishop because some may believe in Medjugorje would be a misunderstanding of the official Vatican and ex-Yugoslavian bishops' statement which makes provision within the lines of full Church obedience for personal belief in the apparitions. The unofficial, personally negative opinion of the local bishop does not bind any member of his diocese or Catholic individual elsewhere to follow his own personal opinion.

Beyond the issue of belief in Medjugorje's authenticity, there is not a single documented account of any direct act of disobedience to a canonically legitimate directive from the local bishop by the Franciscan priests at St. James Parish. Although there have been tensions historically between the local ordinary and the Franciscan Order of this region regarding issues such as parish assignments and custodianship, these issues are entirely irrelevant to the present issue of obedience to the local bishop by the Franciscans at St. James Parish.

Technically speaking, if there had been some acts of disobedience by the local Franciscans, as gravely wrong as this would be in itself, it would not necessarily in itself discount the possibility of authentic apparitions from the Blessed Virgin Mary to the six visionaries. Only with an individual priest who had an immediate relation or effect on the visionaries, for example as a spiritual director, could an issue of disobedience play a relevant role in the discernment of the apparitions themselves. An appropriate Church investigation examines the issue of authenticity based on the moral integrity of the visionaries themselves along with other legitimate intrinsic criteria, and not upon those who may be only geographically close to the reported event.

Moreover, any reports of disobedience to the bishop by Franciscan priests from surrounding parishes should immediately be ruled out as irrelevant, just as it would be inappropriate to accuse a priest from a particular parish of wrongdoing or disobedience based upon a report of inappropriateness or disobedience concerning another parish priest from his surrounding area or diocese.

JUST TOO LONG?

Question Three: The messages of Medjugorje have been going on daily for over twenty-seven years now. Isn't that too long for authentic supernatural messages to take place? Can these apparitions really be true when they've been reportedly happening for so long?

The length of the series of a reported apparition event is not one of the valid criteria the Church uses in examining the issue of authenticity. The Holy Spirit "blows where he wills" (cf. Jn. 3:8), and the Church concentrates on the "what" issue, the essential elements of message contents, general associated phenomena, and spiritual fruits, rather than the peripheral "how long" issue.

While we can look at Church precedence regarding the domain of approved private revelation to get some indication of what is within the boundaries of past apparitions and mystical communications, we still must be careful not to place human or precedence limitations on the "inscrutable ways of God" (cf. Rom. 11:33).

In fact, we do have cases within the Church's mystical tradition where a series of supernatural communications have lasted as long as or even significantly longer than the more than a quarter-century length of the Medjugorje messages. For example, St. Brigid of Sweden (d. 1373), one of the Church's most approved visionaries and mystics, received visions and messages for well over a quarter century. St. Hildegard (d. 1179) received visions from her early childhood, and consistently from age 15 until her death at 83 for a total of sixty-eight years. St. John Bosco (d. 1888) also began receiving visions as a child and continued to have supernatural communications for more than a half century.

More recently, St. Pio of Pietrelcina (1887-1968) experienced consistent supernatural communications which lasted fifty years, including apparitions, visions, locutions, spiritual transports, and the stigmata. Sr. Lucia of Fatima (1908-2005) began receiving apparitions at the age of nine, and then proceeded to receive both apparitions and messages for decades after her original six 1917 Marian apparitions. It is believed that Sr. Lucia continued to receive supernatural communication from Our Lady, which included the supernatural confirmation of the validity of the 1984 world consecration to the Immaculate Heart of Mary by Pope John Paul II, until shortly before her death in 2005 at the age of 97.

Most recently, the Church approved as authentic the Marian apparitions at Laus, France in May, 2008. These apparitions to the 17-year-old French shepherdess, Benoit, lasted consistently from 1164 until 1718, a period of 54 years.

We must be careful not to use incidental criteria, such as the length of the series of the apparitions, as a fundamental reason to validate or invalidate a reported apparition. Keep in mind that the purpose of authentic private revelation is to encourage humanity to live the public revelation of the saving Gospel of Jesus Christ in its fullness of Catholic truth and life. If our contemporary humanity is not responding in general to the overall message of Jesus Christ and the Church, then we should not be surprised when we see an unprecedented increase in apparitions and messages from the Mother of God, the Queen of Prophets, to encourage our world to respond to the saving light of Jesus Christ amidst a world commonly admitted to be experiencing unprecedented spiritual and moral darkness. Perhaps gratitude, rather than skepticism, would be the more appropriate response.

FALSE ECUMENICAL TEACHING?

Question Four: Do the messages reported by the visionaries contain false teachings regarding ecumenism which contradict the official teachings of the Catholic Church's Magisterium? I've heard that one reported message calls for a type of "religious indifferentism" where one religion is as good as another.

The first element the Church considers in evaluating a reported Marian apparition is its message content. Once again, is the reported message in conformity with the faith and moral teachings of the Catholic Church? For the Holy Spirit, who guides the Church, and particularly the papal office of Peter in truth (cf. Mt. 16:15-20), will not contradict himself by revealing a supernatural message to an individual that is contrary to the truth which the same Spirit reveals to the Church (*Catholicism of the Catholic Church*, 67).

The messages of Medjugorje do not contain a single doctrinal teaching that runs contrary to authentic Catholic Magisterial teaching. On the contrary, the Medjugorje messages present in its most fundamental themes the Gospel message of Jesus Christ for faith, prayer, fasting, conversion and peace; as were also expounded upon by the Fathers of the Church. At the same time, the messages convey a contemporary formulation of Catholic teachings which profoundly parallels the teachings of the Second Vatican Council, the postconciliar teachings of the Papal Magisterium, as well as embodying a present-day continuation of the approved Marian messages of Lourdes and Fatima.[1]

---

1 Cf. For example, M. Miravalle, Doctrinal dissertation entitled, *The Message of Medjugorje: A Postconcilar Formulation of Lourdes and Fatima,* May 31, 1984, which was successfully defended at the Pontifical University of St. Thomas (Angelicum) in Rome, and which presented the thesis of the complete conformity of the Medjugorje message with the teachings of the Gospels and the Church Fathers in its foundational elements, and with the Second Vatican Council, its postconciliar teachings, along with the approved messages of Lourdes and Fatima in its developmental themes.

Let us specifically examine the Medjugorje message regarding ecumenism. The message given by the Blessed Virgin states: *"In God's eyes, there are no divisions and there are no religions. You in the world have made the divisions. The one mediator is Jesus Christ. Which religion you belong to cannot be a matter of indifference. The presence of the Holy Spirit is not the same in every Church."*[2] The visionary Mirjana added that the Madonna "deplored the lack of religious unity, especially in the villages. She said that everybody's religion should be respected, and of course, one's own."[3]

This message accurately portrays the Catholic Church's teaching on ecumenism from the Second Vatican Council in its most key components. First, God did not make different religious divisions in the world; man did. Second, the truth of the Holy Spirit does not dwell equally in all religions, and therefore, the religion one belongs to cannot be a matter of indifference. Third, in spite of substantial differences in truth, we should respect all religions in an authentic effort towards eventual unity in the one Body of Christ (*Catechism of the Catholic Church*, 817-822.)

The Fathers of the Second Vatican Council, after discussing the elements of truth and moral life deserving respect in other world religions, confirmed the fullness of truth in Jesus Christ and the Catholic Church:

> The Catholic Church rejects nothing of what is true and holy in these religions. She has a high regard for the manner of life and conduct, the precepts and doctrines, which, although differing in many from her own teachings, nevertheless often reflects a ray of that truth which enlightens all men. Yet she is in duty bound to proclaim without fail, Christ who is the way, the truth, and the life (Jn. 1:6). In Him, in whom God reconciled all things to himself (2 Cor. 5:18-19), men find the fullness of their

---

2 Message of Medjugorje reported between 1981-1983.
3 Ibid.

religious life.[4]

In its decree on Ecumenism, the Second Vatican Council refers to the human elements which have led to division within the Church in a clear parallel to the Medjugorje message on ecumenism, but likewise calls for the restoring of Christian unity in the one Church of Christ:

> The restoration of unity among all Christians is one of the principal concerns of the Second Vatican Council. Christ the Lord founded one Church and one Church only. However, many Christian communities present themselves as the true inheritors of Jesus Christ; all indeed profess to be followers of the Lord but they differ in mind and go their different ways, as if Christ himself were divided. Certainly, such division openly contradicts the will of Christ, scandalizes the world, and damages the holy cause, the preaching of the Gospel to every creature.[5]

Not only do the messages of Medjugorje conform completely to the Church's official teachings, but they reflect the most current expression of the Church's teachings with its emphasis on issues precisely such as ecumenism and the contemporary Church mission of authentic Christian unity.

---

4 Second Vatican Council, Nostra Aetate, n. 2.
5 Second Vatican Council, Unitatis Redintegratio, n. 1.

FALSE VISIONARIES?

Question Five: I've heard that the visionaries were not particularly devout before the apparitions began. How do we know they have not been simply falsifying these apparitions for reasons of their own personal gain?

When the Church examines the "visionaries" or recipients of a reported apparition, they look for evidence of the moral integrity of the individual particularly *from the beginning point of apparitions onward.* The Church does not require a standard of holiness for the visionary, either before the reported supernatural occurrence begins, or even after its beginning. What the Church seeks to establish is the basic moral integrity of the reported visionary, coupled with the question of what level of Christian virtue and integrity does the individual exhibit during the period of reported apparitions as a potential result of the apparition itself. Several Church approved apparitions have included visionaries who were not canonized, but did manifest a fundamental moral honesty and life of Christian virtue.

The Church grants the possibility that God could choose, in his mysterious ways, someone to receive a heavenly message who could be far from Christ or from the Church, and then to experience conversion as a result of the supernatural intervention. Otherwise, how could we make provision for some of the apostles and disciples of Jesus himself, such as St. Matthew or St. Mary Magdalene, whose former lives where not in conformity with the Gospel, but whose later conversion became examples of Christian discipleship for all times.

Therefore it is an authentic moral goodness from the beginning of the reported apparitions, and not so much their past lives or even an exceptional standard of holiness, that commission members of Church investigations look for as essential in evaluating the basic conditions for a possible recipient of heavenly visits or messages.[1]

The six Medjugorje visionaries, Ivanka Ivankovic, Mirjana Dragicevic, Vicka Ivankovic, Marija Pavlovic, Ivan Dragicevic and Jakov Colo, have been under the "public microscope" for most of their adolescent and adult lives. They have been interviewed by a countless number of bishops, priests, religious, theologians, and laity. The overwhelming consensus of public opinion for those who have had direct contact with these six visionaries is a profound respect for their manifest integrity, straightforwardness, and the down-to-earth approach to the Christian life and to their experience as visionaries. Theologians who have interviewed the visionaries have likewise concluded to the same obvious presence of moral integrity and personal authenticity.[2]

Remarkable personal sacrifice rather than personal gain has been the foremost experience of these six people, often at the painful expense of personal privacy and hardship. Daily talks to pilgrims, prayer groups, and healing prayer sessions have been the benchmark of life for the majority of the Medjugorje seers for the last 26 years.

Worthy of particular mention is the Christian witness of Vicka Ivankovic, known for both her extraordinary suffering and her irrepressible smile. Since the apparitions began, Vicka has suffered an inoperable brain cyst, severe spinal pain, and a series of similar physical or spiritual penances, which she joyfully chooses to offer for the conversion of sinners and the salvation of souls. Numerous reports of spiritual and physical healings have come as a result of Vicka's praying over pilgrims, which she does only with the expressed permission of the parish priests. Although exceptional Christian holiness is not a requirement for being a true

---

1 Cf. M. Miravalle, *Private Revelation: Discerning with the Church,* Queenship publications, p. 17. Cf. especially criteria of Pope Benedict XIV for recipients of prophecy, some of whom could theoretically be outside of grace, such as the prophet Balaam and Caiphas.

2 Cf. R. Laurentin and H. Joyeux, *Scientific and Medical Studies on the Apparitions at Medjugorje,* Robert Faricy, S.J., *A Medjugorje Retreat;* Fr. Michael O'Carroll, *Medjugorje: Facts, Documents, Theology: Is Medjugorje Approved?;* M. Miravalle, *Introduction to Medjugorje,* Ch. 1.

visionary, Vicka seems to embody both roles with an inspiring and contagious Christian joy.

Two medical teams, one from Milan and the other from renowned French University of Montpellier, have scientifically examined the visionaries during the time of reported apparitions. Each has independently validated the legitimacy of their state of ecstasy as being in some form of true communication outside of their ordinary time-space experience.[3] These scientific studies also ruled out any possibility of "collective hallucination" and, by deduction, any form of mere human deception of falsification.[4]

3 James Paul Pandarakalam, "Are the Apparitions of Medjugorje Real?" *Journal of Scientific Exploration,* Vol. 15, No. 2, pp. 229-239, 2001. Cf. Laurentin and Joyeux, *Scientific and Medical Studies on the Apparitions at Medjugorje.*
4 Ibid.

ARE THE APPARITIONS
AT MEDJUGORJE AUTHENTIC?

✝

The Medjugorje apparitions possess all the principal characteristics that the Church looks for in manifesting supernatural authenticity. The message contents are in complete conformity with the official doctrinal teachings of the Catholic Church. The phenomena that accompany the messages constitute scientifically validated ecstasy during the apparitions and numerous reports of healings. The visionaries manifest lives of moral integrity and psychological stability. The spiritual fruits from the apparitions have also had a monumental worldwide effect of conversions, returns to the Church and to proper states in life, as well as an extraordinary number of vocations to the priesthood and religious life.

Further credibility is added by the fact that more than 200 bishops, archbishops, and cardinals have visited the site officially, in addition to the many unofficial visits by the shepherds of the Church. In addition, well over 100 bishops, archbishops, and cardinals have publicly expressed their belief in Our Lady's presence in Medjugorje.[1] The spiritual fruits of conversion and spiritual peace have been the ubiquitous testimony of the greater part of the forty million pilgrims who have come to Medjugorje and have responded to the Queen of Peace's call for greater faith, prayer, fasting, conversion, and peace.

1 For the comprehensive list of the name of the cardinals, archbishops and bishops, see last section of the book.

TWO PERSONAL TESTIMONIES

+

Two personal testimonies to the supernatural reality of Medjugorje are worthy of special mention.

On August 14, 1994, I was in Calcutta, presenting talks on the fifth Marian Dogma of Mary Co-redemptrix, Mediatrix and Advocate to six different sections of Missionaries of Charity groups at Mother Teresa's direct request (including two of which Mother herself attended). When I first entered her presence and walked over to the place we would sit and begin talking, I saw a calendar with the image of Our Lady of Medjugorje on its cover hanging on the wall next to us. After a few minutes of enthusiastic conversation with Mother regarding other Marian issues, I pointed up to the calendar and asked her, "Mother, do you believe in Medjugorje?" She responded by putting her finger up to her lips as if to gesture "shhh" or, let us speak quietly of this, and answered, "I asked Our Lady of Medjugorje to come to my first home for the dying in Calcutta, and she did!"

I did not have the courage to further question the future saint, by asking: "How did she come, Mother – in the form of an apparition? A healing?" She simply left the subject with a serene smile on her face.

The second personal testimony comes from Pope John Paul II. Over the course of his blessed pontificate, he had received several of the visionaries in private audience, including a twenty-minute audience with Mirjana in 1987;[1] he had invited numerous bishops and priests to go to Medjugorje and to pray for him there;[2] and the late Cardinal Tomasek had made public the typical comment of John Paul II to inquiring bishops: "If I were not Pope I would like

---

1 Denis Nolan, "John Paul II Believed in Medjugorje," *Mother of All Peoples Marian E-zine,* June 30, 2007.
2 Ibid. Note: I have personally spoken to three American bishops who have the same experience of an encouragement from John Paul II to visit Medjugorje and to pray for him there.

to go to Medjugorje to help at the work with the pilgrims."[3]

We have in incontestable documentation the written words of Pope John Paul II to his lifetime Polish friends, Marek and Sophia Skwarnicki in their personal correspondence (released with their permission), which manifests the saintly Holy Father's personal belief in Medjugorje, and his common spiritual practice of daily pilgriming to Medjugorje in his heart."[4]

For example, in John Paul's letter of December 1992 to the Skwarnicki Family, he writes:

> "I thank Sophia for everything concerning Medjugorje. I, too, go there every day as a pilgrim in my prayers: I unite in my prayers with all those who pray there or receive a calling for prayer from there."[5]

On February 25, 1994, John Paul writes:

> "I guess Medjugorje is better understood these days. This kind of 'insisting' of our Mother is better understood to-day when we see with our very eyes the enormousness of the danger. At the same time, the response in the way of a special prayer—and that coming from people all around the world—fills us with hope that here, too, the good will prevail."[6]

In closing his May 28, 1992, letter to his Polish friends, John Paul reiterates:

> "And now we every day return to Medjugorje in prayer."[7]

---

3 Ibid.
4 "Original Letter Correspondence of Pope John Paul II to Marek and Sophia Skwarnicki," as published in Nolan, *Medjugorje and the Church,* Queenship Publications, pp. 151-147.
5 Ibid., p. 153.
6 Ibid., p. 157.
7 Ibid., p. 155.

In conclusion, we again ask the question: Are the Medjugorje apparitions authentic?

According to the Church's own criteria, the spiritual fruits superabundant throughout the world, and the saintly witnesses and discernments of Pope John Paul II and Blessed Teresa of Calcutta, I believe the only appropriate theological and objective response must be, "Yes. It is authentic. She is real."

—Dr. Mark Miravalle

PART TWO: GOOD FRUITS

THE GOODFRUITS OF BLIND FAITH

It is not a black-and-white matter of choice between Church-grounded theology and blind faith acceptance in discerning the authenticity of a miracle like the daily apparitions of the Blessed Virgin Mary at Medjugorje. Common sense dictates that one cannot stand without the other.

To "prove" the authenticity of this incredible supernatural ongoing event, theology is required to confirm the content, structure and message of the apparitions through adherence to Church doctrine and Holy Scripture. The acceptance of it by individuals requires an act of blind faith beyond the theological foundation. It then produces the good fruits borne out by a usually dramatic spiritual change in daily life and gives witness through a steady, enthusiastic, voluntary conformance to its central message, over an appropriate period of time.

We call this blending of theological acceptance and blind faith spiritual conversion. It takes both whether it's the apparitions at Medjugorje or some other marvelous spiritual miracle.

In the first section, Doctor Mark Miravalle has given us the necessary theology to answer the basic questions of the skeptics, unbelievers and opponents of the Medjugorje apparitions. The objective here is to give added credibility to that theology through personal witness of my own spiritual conversion and that of others.

The stories in this section represent the different levels of spiritual conversion—from total surrender of one's self spiritually and physically, to sudden and/or dramatic transformation of the soul. They are intended to give a generic sample of the great fruits borne by the apparitions over a period of time.

Thousands of similar stories exist like those given here. The good fruits coming from the apparitions at Medjugorje can be likened to the words of St. John the Evangelist who, speaking of the deeds of Jesus, tells us: "But there are also many other things which Jesus did; were every one of them to be written, I suppose that the world itself could not contain the books that would be written." (Jn 21:25).

FROM SKEPTIC TO BELIEVER

-|-

**Without my own first-hand experience in the Medjugorje appari-
tions, I would never have been called to write and speak about
them. For many people, it takes a dramatic mini-miracle to bring
about conversion.**

When I first heard about the apparitions of the Blessed Virgin
Mary taking place in a remote village in Yugoslavia, I didn't believe it professionally or personally.

Professionally, as a newspaper journalist, I was trained to be
a skeptic of everything unless there was definite and substantial
proof. My job as a news reporter was to be adversarial in my
approach to all stories. Such bizarre subjects as apparitions and
other claims of religious supernatural events were all but auto-
matic rejections of belief by journalists.

How was it possible for the Blessed Virgin Mary to be appearing to young, uneducated peasant children, I thought, when
first hearing about Medjugorje. She lived and she died. That was
cold, hard fact. The claim that the Virgin Mary was appearing to
these kids had to be a hoax, mass hallucination or just the wild
antics of teenagers.

Personally, I had never given more than two thoughts to the
Blessed Virgin Mary, noticing her only during the Christmas sea-
son when the traditional crèche scenes were displayed. Nor had
I ever heard of her appearing in apparition. The mention of the
Virgin Mary only brought to my mind thoughts of Catholicism.
As far as I was concerned, she was part of the Catholic Church;
and, as a lukewarm Lutheran Protestant, I wasn't really too fond
of Catholics.

It took a dramatic personal miracle to change me from pro-
fessional skeptic and personal rejecter of anything "Catholic".
After hearing about Medjugorje during a Sunday school class at
my church—and immediately rejecting it as nonsense—my only

interest in it was as a journalist who owned four small weekly newspapers. I thought it might make an interesting article to use sometime during the upcoming Christmas season.

I asked the person who had mentioned it if there were any written works on the subject and she responded by telling me that the friend who told her about it had a recently made video tape about the apparitions. She would see if she could borrow it for me.

A few days later, I decided to view the video tape. It was mid-October 1985, on a Wednesday evening, a date and time I will never forget. With pencil and paper at hand to take notes, I pushed the play button on the video machine to see this "thing about apparitions".

Within minutes of viewing the tape, I knew in my heart that Medjugorje was real; and, I knew that my watching the video was for more than just another story for my newspapers. It immediately became subjective rather than objective for me and I totally forgot about taking written notes.

Halfway through watching the video tape, it showed the young visionaries at the moment of the apparition. As I watched, I suddenly "felt" that the Blessed Virgin Mary was speaking directly to my heart and she was asking me to make the spreading of the Medjugorje apparitions my life's mission. I was literally in physical shock and fell back into my chair mentally thinking, "No, no, you've got the wrong person – I'm not Catholic!"

But I found myself overwhelmed. After watching the tape again, I rendered a weak "Yes, I'll try" answer.

My life was forever changed during the watching of that video and the mission of spreading the story of the Medjugorje apparitions became my all-consuming passion. I sold my businesses and began traveling first in my home state, and then the country and shortly, the entire world.

More importantly, over a period of time, blind faith belief in what I considered to be a "Catholic thing" brought about true spiritual conversion that is my driving force to this day. More than 23 years later, I am still writing and speaking about the apparitions, having authored seven books on them and having traveled to every continent for speaking engagements.

I am now a Christian Catholic, deeply in love with the faith founded by and through the teachings of Jesus Christ. And Mary is no longer just a figure in the crèche scenes of Christmas.

NO GREATER GIFT

As Scripture tells us, there is no greater gift then to lay down one's life for another. I witnessed this act of pure sacrifice on my first pilgrimage to Medjugorje in May 1986. It reinforced in the strongest way the fruits of blind faith generated by the ongoing Medjugorje apparitions.

Traveling with a group of approximately 70 people, we had a wide assortment of "reasons" among us as to why we as individuals were journeying to Medjugorje. I was there to experience for myself what I had felt eight months earlier in the Blessed Virgin Mary's call to make the spreading of the messages my life's mission.

It seemed that I was also the "token" Protestant among 70 Catholics, a fact that would later give credence to the Blessed Virgin's messages that she was not there just for Catholics but for all the children of God. The call to all people of all faiths was just further proof that this was of God. Others had come to renew or recover faith in God, boosted by the startling reports of supernatural phenomena witnessed by those who preceded them in pilgrimage to the village. Many were discovering through the apparitions that God was indeed, *real.*

Several of our pilgrims, like thousands of others who came to Medjugorje, were there hoping for a personal supernatural phenomenon—a miraculous cure of a disease or physical disability. Two of them in particular would easily qualify; both had terminal cancer with only weeks to live.

Carlos, a 70-year-old retired architect was practically hand-carried to Medjugorje by family members, hardly able to walk as he suffered in the last stages of bone cancer. Another pilgrim, John, was also dying of cancer. He was only 50. Both were accompanied by family members praying fervently for that rare opportunity for their loved one to be in the apparition room with the visionaries during the time of the apparition. Cures had happened to others fortunate enough to gain entrance and they were hoping and praying.

Of course thousands of other pilgrims suffering a wide assortment of incurable diseases or conditions were there for the same reason. It made the chances of actually gaining entrance into the apparition room for our fellow pilgrims remote at best. Only a few of the sick were chosen each evening.

It was a battle before every apparition as to who among the ill would be allowed into the cramped space of the small bedroom near the entrance of the rectory that served as the site of the event. Flashes of chaos erupted regularly among the hundreds standing outside the rectory praying the rosary each evening while waiting for the time of the apparition. Hysterical pleadings and wild attempts by some to push into the room interrupted the low thunder of prayer by the masses, only to be rebuffed by several Croatian men who served as voluntary guards for the priest in charge of who among the sick would be let in.

That priest was Slavko Barbaric, a stalwart Franciscan who agonized over each choice. His was the cruelest of jobs, he would tell me later in an interview. No matter whom he chose to be let into the room, there were so many others just as deserving.

We prayed as a group for our two cancer-stricken pilgrims. Several days later, we were informed that one of the two would be allowed into the room. John was the one chosen. His family rejoiced while Carlos' family despaired.

Then, the real miracle took place. John, after a long, angst-ridden meeting with his family, went to Carlos and quietly insisted he take his place in the apparition room. Carlos protested but John remained resolute. He wanted Carlos to take his place. It was his gift to God for allowing him to be in Medjugorje. He had truly found the peace that passes all understanding.

Carlos, with the forceful urging of his family and with a flood of tears from all around, humbly accepted the offered gift. That evening, he entered the apparition room under the watchful protection of Father Slavko and his volunteer guards.

It was a few months later that I learned that Carlos had been totally healed, fully regained his health and had returned to his profession as an architect in his hometown in Baltimore, Maryland.

I further learned that John had died peacefully a short time after returning from Medjugorje. He had given his chance for a possible cure—his life—to a fellow pilgrim.

In actuality, both John and Carlos were healed; Carlos received a full physical healing, while John received the ultimate healing of the soul.

FROM HATRED TO HOPE

✝

What greater witness can there be than that of a lost soul sunk so far into the abyss of darkness that there is no possible escape, who then is dramatically brought into the light at the last possible moment? The story of Goran Cukevic, from the very country where the Medjugorje apparitions are occurring, is but one of thousands that is startling and shocking evidence of the fruits of spiritual conversion.

It had become clear from listening to Goran's story that feelings of hatred had begun festering in him at an early age. It started when his four-year-old younger sister fell out of the fourth-floor window of their apartment and was killed; his younger brother contacted meningitis when he was just a year old and was left deaf and unable to speak; and, his father was away from the family home for long periods of time working as a seaman to support his family as best he could. To top it off, Goran's mother was diagnosed with leukemia.

Each succeeding tragedy weighed the family down and little Goran Cukevic was left to cope on his own. He found solace in friends who were usually older than he and were doing wrong things. He remembers his first conscious act of doing wrong: He took a bar of chocolate from a small nearby store and then lied about it. Within the next two years, Goran was routinely committing such acts. He constantly took money from his mother's purse.

By age 11, Goran was introduced to alcohol by his older companions. It was the beginning of his emerging alcohol-and-drug-infested life. Emboldened by drink, Goran started committing acts that normally he would be afraid of trying, including stealing cars. By 13, he was a hardened delinquent, bordering on a full life of crime.

And then tragedy struck its severest blow: Goran's mother

died. Despite his tough ways, he took her death extremely hard. He wanted to die, too, and he told everyone that he was going to kill himself. On the first anniversary of her death, young Goran attempted suicide. He took a pistol and shot himself in the head. The bullet lodged in his brain in a way that would make the bullet too dangerous to remove.

From that first suicide attempt, life plunged rapidly downhill for Goran. Depression pushed him into more alcohol abuse, eventually leading to marijuana and later to hard drugs. Heroin soon became the new addiction of choice, and, as he would say later, it "opened the doors of hell" for him.

It took a couple of years for the young man's father to discover just how far into the world of darkness his son had sunk. He tried reasoning with him, and when that didn't work, he beat him and screamed at him. Finally, exhausted and at wits end, he resorted to psychiatry. He placed Goran in the psychiatric unit of Split Hospital. This was another lost opportunity for healing, because his son's "friends" would come to visit him and bring him drugs.

Inevitably, Goran ended up in jail. His father decided that it was better for him to remain there rather than work for his release, thinking that this horrible experience might knock some sense into his son's head. But it didn't; He was now a hardened criminal.

Upon Goran's release his father arranged for him to get a job working in the warehouse of the company where he was now employed. Once again, Goran took advantage of the good offered to him and turned it into an easy way to find money for his drugs. He stole everything he could from the warehouse and sold it.

This was too much for his father. The family was disintegrating in the wake of Goran's life of darkness. After his release from yet another stay in jail, Goran's father confronted him. Goran recalled with obvious pain the blunt words of his father: "You have a right to destroy yourself, and I can't stop you. But you don't have the right to destroy the rest of us. You go out there and you take as many drugs as you want to, drink yourself to death if you want to, but don't come back here while you're doing it. Only if you decide to be a man can you come back to this home, and then I'll help you."

At that moment Goran hated his father, hated the whole world, and blamed the whole world for his terrible life.

During the entire period of darkness in his life, Goran never thought of turning to God for help. His family was Catholic, but to him their faith was just a tradition. He had attended catechism lessons and even served as an altar boy, but only because he was made to do it. There was no cry for help to God. His misery would become even worse before poor Goran would reach out through faint remembrance of the Blessed Virgin Mary.

On a freezing cold night in the early winter of 1996, Goran hit rock bottom. He crawled through the broken window of a derelict house and lay down on a piece of cardboard, dropping into a fitful sleep until nightmares awakened him. There was nothing left. He was now 30 years old and had nothing: no family or friends to help him. Rock bottom was the full realization of what he was and where he was.

With nothing left and near death, Goran cried out for help to the Mother of God. He tried to pray, using the only words he could remember: "Hail Mary, holy Mary, pray for us!" It was all coming out wrong, but he didn't care. "Please, Our Lady," he cried through body-wracking sobs, "either take me to you so that I finish this miserable life, or else show me the road to get out of all this!"

For several more days and nights he cried and prayed. Early in the morning of the fourth day, Goran managed to drag himself to a small park near the deserted house. As he watched people come and go, all he could think was, "What will I do?"

Goran watched as a woman approached him. What did she want? Had he robbed her at some point in time? The woman said, "Good morning," and then said she had a problem that possibly Goran could help her with. Goran interrupted her in a weakened, raspy voice saying, "Listen, lady, I have more problems than you can even think of, so just leave me alone."

The woman was undeterred. "I am looking for a young man

who goes by the nickname of "Cuke," she went on. "I was told he hangs around here, and I'm wondering if you could help me find him."

Goran was shocked. Had he heard her right? That was his nickname of the streets. Should he identify himself or would that cause more trouble for him? And then he thought, what more could possibly happen to me? He replied weakly, "That's me, I'm Cuke."

The lady started to cry. She explained that she was the mother of another lost son addicted to drugs and living on the streets who had landed in jail. When she identified her son, Goran realized he wasn't a close friend—just someone he had known on the streets who had ended up in jail. The mother said that every time she went to the jail to visit her son, he would tell her somebody has to help this guy. "He's going to kill himself. Somebody has to find him and help him."

The woman finally managed to get her son out of jail and into Cenacolo Community, the drug rehabilitation center at Medjugorje. She then came looking for Goran. He wouldn't realize it for some time, but his prayers were being answered. How appropriate that the Mother of God would send the mother of another lost son to rescue one of her lost sons.

On arriving in Medjugorje, Goran went to Cenacolo. They had food there and beds. In his mind, this would do until winter was over. He was immediately taken in, and the beginning of a new life started.

Goran soon discovered that life at Cenacolo was harder than all the years he had spent on the streets. For the first time in a long time, he had to actually look at himself in a mirror and see what he had become. He had to come to grips with the fact that he had created the dark life. He didn't know how to speak without cursing, and he had to fight against the pull for drugs. But he had help—other recovering drug addicts, including the son of the mother who had rescued him, who eventually became his best friend. But his fellow addicts had one thing he did not have: family.

One day Goran was asked to show a group from Split around

the facilities, since he was originally from that city. He came into the room to greet the group and was shocked to see his father among them. He could hardly look at him, so filled was he with shame and guilt at what he had done to his family. But his father reached out his hand to him and started to cry. Soon they were embracing and kissing amongst tears of utter joy at seeing each other. Before his father left that evening, Goran promised him that he was going to stay in the community and try to recapture and replace a life of darkness with one of light.

Three years and eight months later, Goran left the community and reentered the world. He had made peace with himself, with the world, and with God through the loving intercession of Gospa.

Life is not easy, and there are heavy obligations. But God had poured out blessings on Goran that he would never have imagined. Shortly after leaving Cenacolo, he met a beautiful young girl who had come to Medjugorje as a pilgrim and stayed. They are now married and have a growing family.

The hatred that dominated the soul of Goran Cukevic has been totally eradicated by the light of God's love.

THE POWER OF APPLYING THE GOOD FRUITS

What power there is in the messages the Blessed Virgin Mary is giving at Medjugorje! Her messages are a complete reiteration of the message of the gospels as given us through the teachings of Jesus. The "power" is derived through adherence to her request that we actively follow the three basic elements of her messages: prayer, fasting and penance. The story of 12-year-old Clare is a strong confirmation of how that holy power works.

Clare struggled down the stairs of the pilgrim home where our group was staying. She moved slowly and with pain, maneuvering the short, aluminum crutches to the landing where her father waited with her wheelchair. She had insisted on descending the stairs on her crutches simply to prove that she could do it. The same was true as we went down another short flight of stairs to the basement where I would be giving my opening talk to our group. Her father hovered anxiously behind her, before retracing his steps to fetch her chair.

Clare and another 12-year-old girl named Makenna had been brought to Medjugorje by family members in hopes of a healing. Makenna suffered from a bipolar disorder with wide mood swings that were affecting the entire family. Clare had cancer of the spine, a far more complicated matter that threatened her young life.

I noticed the determined side of Clare immediately; she was quiet and a little withdrawn, and wanted no special privileges shown her. She disdained anyone paying too much attention to her. Attempts by well-meaning fellow pilgrims to gently hug her were met with noticeable stiffness. Makenna, on the other hand was everywhere talking and animated, making new acquaintances and very much enjoying the attention from the group.

After the talk, I asked our group to pray over these two young girls, led by Father Richard Culver, our spiritual guide, who was a good friend of Clare's family. It was he who had prompted her parents to bring Clare to Medjugorje.

We assembled around the two girls and placed hands on them. We prayed for the Holy Spirit to descend upon them and to bring healing if that was the will of God.

It was the beginning of a powerful healing for the entire group, a phenomenon that regularly occurs to those who make pilgrimage to Medjugorje. It normally starts with the healing of the spirit and the soul—and then the body. With new-found fervor, everyone prayed for everyone else, and especially for the girls. The power of the Medjugorje apparitions was very much in force.

On the last day of our pilgrimage, we chartered a bus and visited a refugee camp about 12 miles from Medjugorje. Visiting refugees is a regular part of all of my pilgrimages to Medjugorje. Its major purpose is not just to bring needed supplies of toiletries, underwear and other items of clothing, along with donations of money for food and medicine to these poor families still living in the camp, but to spend time with them. Its purpose is to give them a few minutes of dignity and respect.

Our visit to the camp, as always, was gut-wrenching, not only for those of us who came to Medjugorje as pilgrims, but also to our guide, Slavenka. She lived through the terror of the horrible, three-plus years of civil war in the early 1990's that led to the destruction of Yugoslavia and the independence of the republics that composed it. Well-educated and one of the best at her job as a Medjugorje guide, Slavenka always had to steel herself for our visit to the refugees. At the same time she was grateful to be part of an effort to help the victims of the war. It was always difficult for her to talk about these times and she was embarrassed for her people and ashamed of the lack of assistance from the government.

As our bus pulled into the camp, people streamed from the tiny aluminum huts that served as houses. Within minutes, the pilgrims were greeting the refugees, distributing candies and other small gifts. Pilgrims were invited by refugees into their homes. It was a reserved but happy intermingling.

It took Joe Murray, Clare's father, several minutes to prepare her wheelchair so that she could join in with the others. She was startled when once settled into her chair, she was suddenly surrounded by children of all ages, who came forward and began hugging her and giving *her* gifts of items that their parents made to sell to visitors to the camp.

Clare at first reacted as she had on the first day of our pilgrimage, when our pilgrims had fussed over her. But overwhelmed by this impromptu outpouring of affection, she soon gave in and accepted the hugs and gifts.

The sight of this young girl confined in a wheelchair had triggered a reverse empathy in the children of the camp. They were expressing exuberant compassion for one of their own, forgetting momentarily their status as refugees. It is a sight I will never forget.

A few months later, I learned from Father Culver that Clare's cancer had regressed. Soon she was walking without the aid of her wheelchair or crutches. After medical examinations, it seemed the cancer of the spine had regressed enough so that this young lady could in the very near future be living a totally normal life.

The power of the healing prayers went even further than the grace of physical healing for Clare. MaKenna, while not healed in the sense of no longer having bipolar disorder, was a far happier and cooperative child upon returning home. As her mother would tell me later in an email exchange, she was still very difficult to handle at times but she had gained so much from her Medjugorje experience.

So had MaKenna's mother, and Clare's father, Joe.

So had the entire group.

PRIESTLY CONVERSION

✝

When considering the good fruits of spiritual conversions taking place at Medjugorje, one does not normally think of the clergy being a part of that process. It is generally assumed for obvious reasons that they are already "converted" spiritually. Yet, priests and religious are first and foremost human, and as such, are subjected to the same demonic attacks and human weaknesses as the faithful. Here is a story of a priestly conversion at Medjugorje that is unique, and yet, similar to hundreds that I have learned about over the years.

Father Ron was in Medjugorje only because, as he would recount in a later interview, it was a chance for a free trip to Europe. Several people from his parish who had made the pilgrimage had convinced him to return with them and to serve as the group's spiritual guide. He had accepted mainly for the opportunity to travel to Europe for the first time. However, before leaving the airport, he was regretting his choice.

It seemed to Father Ron that everyone in the group was asking something of him: would he hear a confession before boarding the flight; could he bless this or that religious object; was it possible for him to explain this or that about the sacraments of the Church. It was not what he expected—or wanted.

Two elderly women of the group, both suffering from chronic medical conditions, immediately became the prominent source of annoyance for the priest. They were so happy and cheerful and nice to him. He wondered why, at their ages and with all of their medical troubles, they were even on the pilgrimage.

The truth was, Father Ron had lost his faith. He did not feel he was a "real" priest anymore. The zeal had eroded several years ago, overwhelmed by the seemingly non-ending duties of a parish priest. He simply went through the motions now, more concerned with things of the world which served as escape from being "Father" to so many people and their problems. The television and VCR were his favorite methods of escape.

Yet when word spread through the diocese that he was going to Medjugorje, a surprising number of fellow priests asked him to pray for them and for the diocese. He promised he would, thinking it was the least he could do—not to mention giving him another rationale for accepting the trip.

Once in Medjugorje, Father Ron was wondering what had prompted him to accept this role as spiritual guide to a group of people so fanatical about their faith. The trip was arduous, long and exhausting. The pilgrim home where they were staying was small with tiny Spartan rooms. Worst of all, there was no television! To top it off, their pilgrimage guide informed the group that first thing in the morning, they would climb Cross Mountain, a standard part of every pilgrimage to Medjugorje. As spiritual guide, Father Ron would lead the group in praying the Stations of the Cross up the mile-long climb.

Grumbling to himself, Father Ron joined the group at the base of the Cross Mountain at 6:30 a.m. They were climbing early to avoid the heat of the mid-summer day. Resigned to the task, he began to organize who would lead sections of the prayers at each station, Suddenly, he noticed the two elderly women near the back of the group. "Wait a minute ladies, surely you're not going to do this. It's too long and difficult. Why don't you wait for us here at the bottom."

The two ladies smiled and said to Father Ron, "Well, we'll go with you for a couple of the stations and then stop if it's too much."

After two stations, Father Ron went to the ladies and insisted they stop and wait right there for the group to finish the climb. "Oh, Father," they answered, "We're fine for now so we'll do another station." Exasperated, he nodded and continued the climb.

By the seventh station, Father Ron noticed that his two elderly pilgrims were trailing far behind. "Please, ladies, stop here. You've done enough."

"Oh, Father, we're just a little slow. We'll be alright."

As the group progressed, Father Ron slowly lost his irritation with the ladies. In fact, he thought it was incredible that they had made it this far. He shook his head in silent admiration of their effort.

The scene continued to be played out as the group progressed up the mountain resting briefly at each praying of the Stations with the two ladies bringing up the rear—until they all had reached the summit where the huge cross overlooked the valley below.

Something had happened to Father Ron during the final stages of the ascent. He thought of his priesthood and how it had disintegrated to a point of nonexistence. He thought of the two women and how they struggled all the way to the top, exhausted but so happy.

Father Ron scrambled to the base of the cross and knelt down, intending to pray for his brother priests and the diocese as promised. But something happened as he began his prayer. "Oh, my God, what have I done with my priesthood?"

Tears flowed down his cheeks as years of failure filled his thoughts. He prayed and asked forgiveness. After awhile, a peace filled him as he knew he was meant to be here, not for a European vacation but to rediscover his vocation. He then made a vow on the spot to get rid of his television and VCR as soon as he returned home.

The group waited on their priest, each finding a little niche to find the peace that passes all understanding. Finally they reassembled and prepared to start down the mountain. But before starting down, Father Ron went to the two elderly ladies. "Look, girls, I know this was a rough climb for you. Let me help you down." Smiling and thankful, each took an offered arm and Father Ron led them to the bottom of the mountain.

The majority of the remaining days of the pilgrimage for Father Ron were spent in the confessionals hearing as he would later state, "The most powerful confessions I have ever heard." Many priests journeying to Medjugorje on pilgrimage would eventually state the same thing.

Conversion for the clergy at Medjugorje predominantly comes

through rediscovery of the grace of vocation, and rediscovery of the great grace of the sacraments of the Church—especially the Sacrament of Confession.

Father Ron did indeed get rid of his television and VCR and is now fulfilling his role as priest to the limit.

THE ULTIMATE GOOD FRUITS STORY

There are thousands of stories out of Medjugorje concerning physical healing. What greater good spiritual fruit than that which the eye can behold: a true, authentic physical healing of a person with a crippling physical condition or terminal disease.

One of the most popular stories of physical healing among followers of the Medjugorje apparitions is that of Rita Klaus, a Pennsylvania school teacher who after 25 years of crippling Multiple Sclerosis, was physically healed overnight. She hadn't gone to Medjugorje but only read a book about the apparitions and instantly believed, giving her hope and strength to focus her life on spirituality.

The incredulity of Rita's story is heightened by the fact that Rita had both knees surgically altered so that she could be fitted with special braces to assist her in walking. Most of her waking time was spent in a wheelchair. The knees were whole and completely normal on the morning of June 18, 1986, a day after Rita, inspired by Medjugorje, had prayed for God to heal her of "what ever she needed to be healed of." In fact, her MS was completely eradicated. Rita now spends a good deal of time giving witness to her mystical healing.

As incredible as Rita's story is, there is another which stands with hers as a healing miracle of the first magnitude. Both stories are powerful beacons of the good fruits flowing from the messages of Medjugorje.

Colleen Willard, from Chicago, Illinois, suffered from an inoperable brain tumor, and 15 other major ailments. There was something called Hashimoto's thyroiditis, there was myofascial fibromyalgia, severe osteomalacia, critical adrenal insufficiency - and so many complications beyond these that Colleen could hardly hold her head up and was confined to a wheelchair and canes for mobility when she had the strength.

Hearing about the miracle of Medjugorje, John and Colleen were determined to go, but none of the major airlines wanted her to fly the long journey to Medjugorje because of her complicated and dangerous medical conditions. Nor did good friends and tour leaders, Jack and Gail Boos, who have been taking pilgrims to Medjugorje for a long time. Yet, medical clearance, near as miraculous, came through; Jack and Gail reluctantly agreed to take Colleen and husband John and then supported them in every way.

The journey was difficult and long causing prolonged suffering to Colleen. She could not stand to be even lightly touched without great pain. After nearly 24 hours, John and Colleen arrived at the pilgrim home where they would be staying.

Early the following morning, September 3, 2003, the owner of the home transported Colleen and John to visionary Vicka's home, where she was already speaking to pilgrims. Hundreds crowded together in the small court yard below the steps where Vicka was speaking. Colleen was maneuvered into place in the court yard after much turmoil trying to get those pilgrims who were already there to allow her a space. They leaned in on Colleen causing more pain, and John and the other pilgrims from their group actually feared for her life.

Suddenly, Vicka stopped speaking, looked directly at Colleen and then began motioning for the crowd to make room for her to approach Colleen. As she approached, Vicka smiled broadly and kept saying in English, "Praise God! Praise God!" she then laid hands on Colleen and prayed over her for nearly ten minutes. Colleen would later report that she felt a constant feeling of heat coming from Vicka's hands.

There was stunned silence; then a loud buzzing of conversation, the languages of Italian, Croatian, English and others intermingling. The Croatian man who had brought Colleen to the apparition with the help of the group led her away to his automobile and immediately drove her to the church to attend the English-speaking Mass.

Colleen sat in her wheelchair in the rear of the church, still tingling from the experience with Vicka. During the consecration of the gifts, she felt as though Jesus was asking her if she wanted to be healed. In total humility, Colleen simply thought, so similar to what Rita Klaus had thought, to be healed of whatever stood in the way of her unconditional love and service to Jesus. Again, there was a flash of heat that went through her and within minutes, she was standing and praying in thanksgiving.

Upon returning to the house after the Mass, Colleen Willard felt completely well, with no pain anywhere. Before long, she was walking around without medical restriction, in amazement to herself and the group. That evening when the man of the house returned and found Colleen and John literally dancing around, he became highly upset, thinking that a cruel trick had been played on him. It took awhile for his wife and others to explain to him what had happened. Soon he was in tears of joy and dancing around with the others.

All of her medical doctors fully examined Colleen when she returned to the states. They found no traces of any of the 16 diseases and conditions that had rendered her crippled for so long—including the inoperable brain tumor. It was, without doubt, a miracle grace of the first magnitude. But for Colleen the real miracle was not the healings, but the fact that the entire episode drew her closer to Jesus on the cross.

EPILOGUE

Colleen Willard's story is truly a miracle brought about by the apparitions at Medjugorje, as are all of the others. The theology applied in the opening part of the book gives credibility beyond just the good fruits. The apparition of the Blessed Virgin Mary taking place daily (and continuing as of this writing into its 28th year) is, in my opinion, the greatest event of our time.

Medjugorje is truly a place of miracles - everything from such incredible physical healings to the millions of spiritual healings. It is the reason many of us have made the spreading of its messages our mission for life. We hope that the content of this work will help bring others to full belief.

We close with this legendary statement purportedly made by Saint Frances: For those who believe, no proof is necessary; for those who do not, no proof will suffice.

In late June 2008, the Vatican announced that it will form a new commission to investigate the apparitions, taking decisive action on earlier published statements made in May 2008. This is an unprecedented move by the Vatican concerning the investigation of claimed apparitions. We pray that this commission, upon traveling to Medjugorje and experiencing its grace, will reach the same conclusion as the more than 40 million pilgrims who have made pilgrimage to the little village of Medjugorje.

BISHOPS WHO HAVE VISITED MEDJUGORJE ON PILGRIMAGE:

-|-

Thousands of priests have visited the apparition site of Medjugorje and found "conversion" of varying degrees similar to the story of Father Ron described in the last section. Additionally, hundreds of cardinals, archbishops and bishops, representing every continent, have visited the site in order to form for themselves a judgment. (The list does not include names of some bishops and cardinals who chose to visit Medjugorje unofficially.)

We publish this list of clergy who have visited Medjugorje as solid proof that the phenomenon has and continues to touch hearts not only of the faithful but of the hierarchy of the Church itself.

Bishop Sebastian Thekethecheril, the diocese Vijayapuram, Kerala, (India)
Archbishop Luigi Bommarito, Archbishop Emeritus of Catania (Italy)
Bishop Joseph Leo Charron, Bishop Emeritus of Des Moines (USA)
Bishop Domenico Sigallini, of Palestrina (Italy)
Bishop László Bíró, Auxiliary Bishop of the Diocese Kalocsa-Kecskemét (Hungary)
Bishop Brendan Oliver Comiskey, SS.CC., Bishop Emeritus of Ferns (Ireland)
Archbishop Estanislao Esteban Karlic, Archbishop Emeritus of Paraná, and former president of the Episcopal Conference of Argentina (Argentina)
Bishop Claude Frikart, Auxiliary Bishop Emeritus of Paris (France)
Bishop Bernardo Cazzaro, Archbishop Emeritus of Puerto Montt (Chile)

Bishop Boulos Emile Saadé, Maronite Bishop of the Batroun Diocese (Lebanon)

Bishop Emilio Ogñénovich, Archbishop Emeritus of Mercedes-Luján (Argentina)

Bishop Geevarghese Divannasios Ottathengil, Malankarese Bishop of Battery (Kerala, India)

Cardinal Timothy Manning, Los Angeles, California (USA)

Cardinal Emmanuel Wamala, Kampala (Uganda)

Cardinal Jean Margeot, Port Louis (Mauritius)

Cardinal Ruiz Bernardino Echeverria, Quito (Ecuador)

Cardinal Giuseppe Uhac, Cong. for Evangelization (Vatican)

Cardinal Franjo Kuharic, Archbishop of Zagreb (Croatia)

Cardinal Corrado Ursi, Naples (Italy)

Cardinal Maradiaga Oscar Rodriguez, Tegucigalpa (Honduras)

Archbishop Girolamo Prigione, Apostolic Delegate (Mexico)

Archbishop Frane Franic, (retired), Split (Croatia)

Archbishop Gorny Kazimierz, Krakow (Poland)

Archbishop Patrick Flores, San Antonio, Texas (USA)

Archbishop Philip Hannan, New Orleans, Louisiana (USA)

Archbishop Giuseppe Casale, Foggia (Italy)

Archbishop Donat Chiasson, Moncton (Canada)

Archbishop Sablan Apuron, Guam, (Oceania)

Archbishop George H. Pearce, Suva (Fiji Islands)

Archbishop Pantin Anthony, Trinidad (W. Indies)

Archbishop Joachim Johannes Degenhardt, Paderborn (Germany)

Archbishop Edwardo G. Amaral, Maceio (Brazil)

Archbishop Jose Hipolito De Morais, Lorena (Brazil)

Archbishop Jean Chabbert, Perpignan (France)

Archbishop Gabriel Gonsum Ganaka, Jos, Plateau State (Nigeria)

Archbishop George Eder, Salzburg (Austria)

Archbishop Emilio Ognenovich, Mercedes-Lujan (Argentina)

Archbishop Francisco Spanedda, Oristano (Italy)

Archbishop Franc Perko, Belgrade (Yugoslavia)

Archbishop S. Fumio Hamao, Pres., Bishops Conf. of Japan

Archbishop Fabio B. Tirado, Manizalesa (Columbia)

Archbishop Andre Fernand Anguile, (Gabon)
Archbishop Jan Sokol, Trnava, Bratislava (Slovakia)
Archbishop Edwin O'Brien, US Armed Forces (USA)
Archbishop Jose Dimas Cedeo Delgado, Pea Blanca (Panama)
Archbishop Farhat Edmond, (Apostolic Nuncio) (Slovenia)
Archbishop Paul Kim Tchang-Ryeol, Seoul (South Korea)
Archbishop Nicodemus Kirima, Nyeria (Kenya)
Archbishop George Riachi, Tripoli (Libanon)
Archbishop Leonard HSU, (retired) Taipei (Taiwan)
Archbishop Antoun Hamid Mourani, (Maronite) Damascus (Syria)
Archbishop Luigi Bommarito, (retired) Catania (Italy)
Archbishop Hieronymus H. Bumbun, Pontianak (Indonesia)
Archbishop Gaetano Allibrandi, Papal Nuncio, Dublin (Ireland)
Archbishop Armondo Bortolasio, Papal Nuncio (Syria)
Archbishop Enrico Masseroni, Mondovi (Italy)
Archbishop Rubén Héctor di Monte, Mercedes-Luján (Argentina)
Archbishop Dr. Franc Kramberger, Maribor (Slovenia)
Archbishop Tomasz Peta, Maria Santissima, Astana, (Kazakhstan)
Archbishop Harry Flynn, Saint Paul/Minneapolis, Minnesota (USA)
Bishop Joseph Fernando, President of Episcopal Conf. (Sri Lanka)
Bishop Anton Hofman, (retired) Munich (Germany)
Bishop Damian Kyaruzi, Bukoba, (Tanzania)
Bishop Salvatore Boccaccio, Frosinone, (Aux Bishop, Rome) (Italy)
Bishop Domenico Sigalini, Palestrina (Italy)
Bishop John E. M. Terra, Brasilia (Brazil)
Bishop Jimenez Lazaro Perez, Halisco, (Mexico)
Bishop Giulio Calabrese, Papal Nuncio (Argentina)
Bishop Antonius Hofmann, Passau (Germany
Bishop Christian Werner, Eca, Vienna (Austria)
Bishop Tonino Bello, Molfetta (Italy)

Bishop Nicholas D'Antonio, New Orleans, LA (USA)
Bishop Carl A. Fisher, Los Angeles, California (USA)
Bishop Michael Pfeifer, San Angelo, Texas (USA)
Bishop Francis A. Quinn, Sacramento, California (USA)
Bishop Sylvester William Treinen, (retired) Boise, Idaho (USA)
Bishop Stanley Ott, Baton Route, Louisiana (USA)
Bishop Henry Joseph Kennedy, Armidale, New S.W. (Australia)
Bishop Thomas O'Connell, Los Angeles, Calif. (USA)
Bishop J. Carboni, Macerata (Italy)
Bishop Jose Gabriel Diaz Cueva, Guayaquil (Ecuador)
Bishop L. Graziano y Antionelli, San Miguel (El Salvador)
Bishop Seamus Hegarty, Derry (Ireland)
Bishop Paolo Hnilica S.J., Rome (Italy)
Bishop Murilo Krieger, Ponta Grossa (Brazil)
Bishop Myles McKeon, Bunbury (Australia)
Bishop Thomas McMahon, Brentwood (England)
Bishop Gratian Mundadan, Bijnor (India)
Bishop John Baptist Odama, Nebbi (Uganda)
Bishop M. Quedraogo, Quahigouya (Burkina Faso)
Bishop Mukombe Timothee Pirigisha, Bukavu (Zaire)
Bishop Matthias Chimole, Lilongwe (Malawi)
Bishop Antonio R. Tobias, San Fernando (Philippines)
Bishop Daniel Tomasella, Marilia (Brazil)
Bishop Severiano Potani, Solwezi (Zambia)
Bishop Hilario Chavez Joya, Casas Grande (Mexico)
Bishop Santana Hermin Negron, San Juan (Puerto Rico)
Bishop Mazzardo Angelico Melotto, Solola (Guatemala)
Bishop Mauriche Chequet, Ottawa (Canada)
Bishop Juan Rodolfo Laise, San Luis (Argentina)
Bishop Manuel Menendez, San Martin (Argentina)
Bishop Lahaen Petrus Frans, Sakania (Zaire)
Bishop Aloysio Jose Leal Penna, Bauru (Brazil)
Bishop Paolo Afonso, (Brazil)
Bishop George Henry Speltz, St. Cloud, Minnesota (USA)
Bishop Janos Penzes, Subotica (Yugoslavia)
Bishop Vitalis Djebarus, Bali, (Indonesia)

Bishop Patrick Quenon, Manila (Philippines)
Bishop Ricardo Ramirez, Las Cruces, New Mexico (USA)
Bishop Armando Ochoa, El Paso, Texas (USA)
Bishop Raymond Mpezele, Livingston, (Zambia)
Bishop Jean-Louis Jobidon, (retired), Mzuzu (Malawi)
Bishop Bonaventura da Gangi (Italy)
Bishop Francis Paul McHugh, Ontario (Canada)
Bishop Thomas Connolly, Baker, Oregon (USA)
Bishop Homero Leite Meira, Irece (Brazil)
Bishop Paetau Luis Maria Estrada, Izabal (Guatemala)
Bishop Serafino Faustino Spreafico, Grajau (Brazil)
Bishop Andre Richard, Bathurst (Canada)
Bishop John Mone, Glasgow (Scotland)
Bishop Donald William Montrose, Stockton, California (USA)
Bishop Domingos Gasbriel Wisniewski, Apucarana (Brazil)
Bishop Daniel Nunez, Chiriqui (Panama)
Bishop John Jobst, Broome (W. Australia)
Bishop Joseph Devine, Motherwell (Scotland)
Bishop Nicola De Angelis,Toronto, Ontario (Canada)
Bishop Michael Pearse Lacey, Toronto, Ontario (Canada)
Bishop Gilbert Aubry, St. Denis, Le Reunion (France)
Bishop Roman Danylak, Toronto, Ontario (Canada)
Bishop Basil Filevich, Saskatoon, Saskatchewan (Canada)
Bishop Sebastian, Olinda (Brazil)
Bishop P. Arokiaswamy, (India)
Bishop Agostinho Kist, Diamantino (Brazil)
Bishop Lorenzo Castellani, Rome (Italy)
Bishop Barraza Isidoro Quinones, Mazatlan (Mexico)
Bishop André-Mutien Léonard, Namur (Belgium)
Bishop Paul Bakyeng, (Uganda)
Bishop Carrero Raul Horacio Scarrone, Florida (Uruguay)
Bishop Patrick Power, Canberra (Australia)
Bishop John Dew, Wellington, (New Zealand)
Bishop Girard Dionn, Edmonson, New Brunswick (Canada)
Bishop Adelio Giuseppe Tomasin, Quixada (Brazil)
Bishop Silverio J. Paulo de Albuquerque, Feira de Santana

(Brazil)
Bishop Albin Malysiak, (Poland)
Bishop Kenneth D. Steiner, (auxiliary) Portland, Oregon (USA)
Bishop Louis Kebreau, Hinche (Haiti)
 Bishop Joseph Lafontant, Port-au-Prince (Haiti)
Bishop Victor Maldonado, (Ecuador)
Bishop German Pavon Puente, Tulcano (Ecuador)
Bishop Carlos Altamirano, (auxiliay) Quito (Ecuador)
Bishop Tadeusz Werno, Koszalina (Poland)
Bishop Michael Marshall, (Anglican) (England)
Bishop Joseph Mugeny Sabiti, (Uganda)
Bishop Christopher Kakooza, (Uganda)
 Bishop Stanislas Lukumwena Lumbala, Kole (Congo)
 Bishop Jose de Jesus Nunez Viloria, (retired) Guyana (Venezuela)
Bishop L. Bataclan, (Philipines)
Bishop Robert Rivas, Kingstown (Caribbean)
Bishop Franziskus Eisenbach, (auxiliary) Mainz (Germany)
Bishop Waldemar Chavez de Aranjo, Sao Joao del Rei (Brazil)
Bishop Kauneckas Jonas, (auxiliary) Telsiai (Lithuania)
Bishop Janez Moretti, (Apostolic Nuncio) Brussels (Belgium)
Bishop Joseph Das, Berhampur (India)
Bishop Florencio Olvera Ochaoa, Tabasco (Mexico)
Bishop Leo Drona, San Jose (Philippines)
Bishop Nestor Carino, Secretary of Bishops' Conf., (Philippines)
Bishop Cirilo Almario, (retired) Malolos (Philippines)
Bishop José Antûnez de Mayolo, Ayacucho (Peru)
Bishop Jean-Claude Rembaga, Bambari (Central Africa)
Bishop Mario Cecchini, Fano-Fossombrone - Cagli Pergola
(Italy)
Bishop Irynei Bilyk, (Byzantine rite) Buchach (Ukraine)
Bishop Hermann Raich, Wabag (Papua New Guinea)
Bishop Matthias Ssekamanya, Lugazi (Uganda)
Bishop Denis Croteau, Mc Kenzie, Northwest Territories
(Canada)
Bishop Jérôme Gapangwa Nteziryayo, Uvria (Congo)
Bishop Nguyen Quang Tuyen, Bac Ninh (Vietnam)

Bishop Silas S. Njiru, Meru (Kenya)
Bishop Julio Ojeda Pascual, San Ramon (Peru)
Bishop Gerard Anton Zerdin, San Ramon (Peru)
Bishop Jean-Vincent Ondo, Oyen (Gabon)
Bishop Ricardo Guerra (vicar) Valencia (Venezuela)
Bishop Salvador Pineiro Garcia-Calderon, Lima (Peru)
Bishop Gerard Ndlovu, (retired) Umzimkulu (South Africa)
Bishop Dr. Ludwig Schwarz, (auxiliary) Vienna (Austria)
Bishop Donal Mc Keown, (auxiliary) Down and Connor
(Ireland)
Bishop Abilio Ribas, Sao Tome and Principe (Africa)
Bishop Jesus a Cabrera, Alaminos (Philippines)
Bishop Thomas L. Dupre, Springfield, Massachusetts (USA)
Bishop Tarcisio Ziyaye, Malawi (Africa)
Bishop Bernardo Witte, Conception (Argentina)
Bishop Bruno Tommasi, (retired) Lucca (Italy)
Bishop Francisco VIII, (retired) Huambo (Angola)
Bishop Mauro Parmeggiani, Rome (Italy)
Bishop Joseph Oyanga, Lira (Uganda)
Bishop Adalbert Ndzana, Mbalmayo (Cameroon)
Bishop William Ellis, Curacao, Neth. Antilles (Caribbean)
Bishop Stanislaus Szyrokoradiuk, Kiev (Ukraine)
Bishop Johannes Dyba, Fulda (Germany)
Bishop Dominic Su, Sibu (Borneo)
Bishop Bernard Joseph Flanagan, Worcester (USA)
Bishop Timothy Joseph Harrington, Worcester (USA)
Bishop Franjo Komarica, Banja Luka (Bosnia Hercegovina)
Bishop Kazimierz Nycz, Krakow (Poland)
Bishop Deogratias Byabazaire, Hoima (Uganda)
Bishop J. Faber MacDonald, Saint John, New Brunswick
(Canada)
Bishop M. Wiwchar, Byzantine Eparchy of Chicago (USA)
Bishop Francesco Mirabella, Palermo (Italy)
Bishop Georges Lagrange, Gap (France)
Bishop Pierre R. DuMaine, San Jose, California (USA)
Bishop Augustine Harris, Emeritus of Middlesborough,

(England)
Bishop Zbigniew J. Kraszewski, Warsaw-Praga (Poland)
Bishop Carvalheria Marcelo Pinto, Guarabire (Brazil)
Bishop Mario Zanchin, Fidenza (Italy)
ishop Ramirez C. Talavera, Coatzacoalcos -Veracruz (Mexico)
Bishop Moged Elhachem, Be El ' Ahhahmar (Lebanon)
Bishop Frederick Dranuba, Arua (Uganda)
Bishop Guiseppi Varelanga, Salerno (Italy)
Bishop Domenico Pecile, Vicar, St. John Lateran Basilica, Rome
Bishop Dominique Rey, Toulon (France)
Bishop Jose Domingo Ulloa Mendieta, Panama (Panama)
Bishop Thomas Msusa, Zomba (Malawi)
Bishop Allan Chamgwera, (retired), Zomba (Malawi)
Bishop Remi Joseph Gustave Saint-Marie, Dedza (Malawi)
Bishop I. J. Darwish, Eparch, Melchite Rite (Aust. & New
Zealand)
Bishop Jose Luis Azcona Hermoso, Mrajo ((Brazil)
Bishop G. Mar Divannasios Ottathengil, Bathery, Kerala (India)
Bishop Lazaro Perez, De Autlan Jalisco (Mexico)
Bishop Daniel E. Thomas (auxiliary) Philadelphia, PA (USA)
Bishop Antal Majnek, Mukachevo (Ukraine)
Bishop Robert W. Finn, Kansas City-St. Joseph (USA)

(Used with permission by Denis Nolan, author of "Medjugorje
and the Church", 4th edition, Qeenship Publishing, pp. 36 – 45)